The Magical Message of Success

I0493608

by Dan Moskel

ISBN-13:
978-1497560772

Other Books by Dan Moskel

- *Entrepreneur Bible To Riches: The Gospel of Wealth Attraction*

- *Video Marketing for Entrepreneurs*

- *Email Marketing That Works ... So You Don't Have To*

- *How To Create a Website Easy Button: Earn Money Online with Google AdSense, Amazon, Your Business, and More*

- *SEO Training Manual - The 10 Golden Steps To Shower In Search Engine Traffic*

- *The Blueprint To Affiliate Marketing: Revealed My Exact Million Dollar Earning Strategies Tips and Tricks*

Table of Contents

Chapter 1. In The Beginning

Look, this is not a book filled with metaphysical feel good B.S. or positive thinking. For I've yet to witness an athlete, upon scoring the game winning shot, stroll over to the sidelines, wipe a bead of sweat from his forehead, look in the camera and say:

"You know Verne, it was all because of that positive thinking I did in the off-season."

You see, in our brave new economy the rules have changed. No longer, could Benjamin Franklin turn the wheels of commerce, with Poor Richards Almanac.

And until we hear Donald Trump say the key to his success constructing magnificent skyscrapers is positive thinking. Let's just say it's a good thing, and leave it at that.

You see I grew up in the church the son of a preacher man, and there is little else, that gets me upset than the so called leaders intentionally leading the herd down a delusional path, of leprechauns, riding unicorns along rainbows.

It's nauseating, certainly, you've heard visiting the Vatican today, is like riding shotgun in a convertible along Hollywood Boulevard with Lloyd from the HBO show, Entourage.

Look, how else can you explain politicians pandering to the idea of fairness and in America of all countries, one of the wealthiest societies. You see much of what you've been told about success and wealth is pure unadulterated baloney!

These ideas of fairness, inequality, or just being more moral and deserving of success, sure they sound nice, but I've yet to hear of success and wealth beating a path to any nice, moral, and deserving people's front door.

After all, drug dealers, gun runners, and criminals can amass extravagant amounts of wealth.

Warning

Yes, a warning. This book will offend the meek, for it is filled with all the dirty little secrets of success, that others are too timid to share.

It will fly in the face of what you've been told growing up and it will challenge many of your current long held beliefs about success and wealth. It may seem illogical, and impractical, at first.

It will be painful, and your first instinct will be to slam these pages shut, and go running under your covers, like a 13 year old little girl after her first break up, whimpering "no, no, no, it's just can't be."

Let me first briefly share my qualifications, so that you will take my words seriously.

While the talking heads on TV have been banging their drum about our great recession, unemployment, and George Bush's last apocalyptic passage of gas, starting from zero financial resources, no silver spoons, or lucky breaks, I've climbed up as a college dropout, to earn millions of dollars working part time from home.

I've traveled the world, from staying at the Wynn in Las Vegas to see Tiesto perform live, to flying out to New York City to attend March Madness in Madison Square Garden, down to riding horseback through the jungles of Belize, off to feeding Elephants in the bustling streets of Bangkok.

You may have even seen me appear on national TV in my own infomercial, on ESPN, MTV, VH-1, Comedy Central to name but a few.

Just like in the movie the Matrix, Keanu Reeves was given the choice of the red pill or the blue pill, right now this moment, your faced with the same decision. For the time is upon you to cast off the heavy chains of false belief, that money goes to scarcity, lack, or need.

For that is blasphemy, and as well thought out as the belief that because you helped carry in little Ms. Jackson groceries this week, and haven't had any immoral thoughts lately ... Gee shucks, it's gotta be your turn to win the lottery.

Sure Homer, I've even been visualizing it.

But if your one of the few, brave, courageous souls, buckle, up and get ready to rise to the top. For our first tale together begins with the Hershey Milk Chocolate Bar.

Go now and grab a copy your free bonus gift of the 12 week success course at DanMoskelUniversity.com

Chapter 2. Hershey Milk Chocolate Bar

If you were to ask the average Joe on the street, how chocolate came to be in our country? He would assuredly tell you it was Milton Hershey, and the Hershey Milk Chocolate Bar. He may even be able to tell you how the award winning ration D Chocolate Bar, became a symbol of democracy during World War 2.

You see, I bet he would even be able to tell you about the Milton Hershey School for orphans. He may even share with you how Milton, was a staunch supporter of the little guy, the worker, and even how Milton went on a hiring, building, and spending spree during the Great Depression.

But he wouldn't tell you, that Milton had failed miserably and went broke with 2 candy businesses prior to his first success. He also wouldn't be able to tell you that this first success came with caramels and not chocolate. Only later, in his career did Milton risk his fortune to bring chocolate to the masses, prior to this, chocolate was only consumed by the ultra rich.

Look, the road of success is not a smooth, or easy road. In fact, it is quite the opposite. But, others only judge what they see, which are your successes.

Very few folks, know that Milton Hershey stopped going to school at 13, or that he lost a fortune in the stock market, or that he built a 170 room hotel that was a spectacular disappointment.

They will however, will be able to tell you about the lives he impacted with his school for orphans, the happiness he continues to bring to the masses with his chocolate bars, and how he continues to influence people with his life, today, yesterday, and tomorrow.

There are 3 great stories that sum up success in life, and Milton Hershey. The first is with his 170 room hotel, when one day he was strolling through the lobby and asked how many guests they had that night, when he was told, just 12. He said, we better give those 12 folks an amazing experience.

You see Milton, didn't go bemoaning bad luck, failure, or saying woe is me that they only had 12 guests. He choose the bright side of the situation, and said lets do a good job, and let's get on with the next task of the day, because I'm sure the next project will do better.

The other story is late in Milton's life, he was still experimenting with confections, and encouraging his nurses to try his latest creations. He created celery, carrot, and potato ice cream, which didn't go over too well, but a surprising success was his beet sorbet.

I'm sure you've heard it before, but we must approach life, as an experiment, just like Milton. Never, stop trying new things, new solutions, and new ways of achieving success.

It's moving to hear graduates of Milton's school, say they would drop to their knees in gratitude for what he did in their lives. You see, even if you don't have as ambitions aims, as

Milton Hershey, you can take a lesson from his life.

If at first you don't succeed, try, try, and try again. This isn't a license to act foolishly with your life, but if you listen to what others tell you, or even fail, even twice like Milton did, and if it's in pursuit of a worthy goal, it only means greater effort is required for achievement!

Anything worth having, is worth working for. These moments the herd call failure, are the moments where success is built! Without failure, setback, and adversity, then enduring success couldn't ever be achieved!

Failure is not only a prerequisite to success it is an ongoing part of success, including monetary setbacks, relationship mistakes, and even the herd's opinion of you.

Success in life, is just like success in any arena. It's about creating the good life, filled with value, and much more than, simply the love of money. It's about continuously using your effort to produce fruitful results, and helping other people do the same!

It's about putting your life together across the board with your career, your spouse, your kids, and everyone that crosses paths with you, along your journey of life. And listening to the wise men that came before us, including Emerson, who said he came across two paths in the road, and choose the one less traveled.

He didn't build a camp, and cry because he didn't know which path to take, or how to get started. Emerson, did exactly what you have to do. He put one foot in front of the other, and acted in the face of fear. This is courage.

You don't need to know steps 3, 4, and 5, if you don't know how to do the first two steps.

You see, working to achieve your dreams, is just like learning math, you have to first learn addition and subtraction, before you can learn how to multiply, and divide. Heck, you can start with steps 3, 4, and 5 ... just so long as you get started, TODAY!

Dan Kennedy, says:

"The act of taking action is in and of itself a magnet for opportunity and wealth."

Stay focused on todays, steps and don't even worry about tomorrows steps, until you get there. After all, if you don't do what you need to do today, you won't be in a position to take advantage of a bigger and better opportunity tomorrow.

Mark Twain said: "Twenty years from now, you will be more disappointed by the things you didn't do, than by the ones you did do."

Chapter 3. Get Skills

The plain truth is success requires no formal education! It does require skills.

Did you know many successful entrepreneurs feel inadequate because they don't have an alphabet soup certificate of intelligence, framed and hanging on a wall in their office, or a mortgage in student loans to repay?

Frank Kern, tells the story of working a menial fast food job, and former high school classmates coming home from medical school, and law school for Christmas break, and upon seeing him saying: "Frank, what are you up to these days?"

And Frank would have to respond with:

"DUDE, I'm obviously the fry guy ... what else do you think I'm doing standing behind the counter!"

An associate of mine, now a retired attorney, says a few years after graduating law school, he "woke up" and realized, a 90 minute commute to work, to be a "Dilbert cubicle attorney" wasn't what he had in mind. My family physician works a second job.

Did You See The Movie Tommy Boy, With Chris Farley?

There is a scene with David Spade picking up Tommy Boy from the airport, upon Tommy's graduating college. David Spade makes some hilarious jabs at Tommy Boy or Chris Farley, for taking 7 years to graduate from college.

But, the plain truth shows us this is the path of success as an entrepreneur. Surely, you've heard the saying about how A students work for C students. Well it took me almost 10 years to escape college with my bachelors degree. But, I've also appeared on national TV in my own infomercial, earned a very affluent income from home, and created a career out of thin air, and I'm not alone!

Did you know there are a plethora of uneducated BILLIONAIRES, not mere millionaires, but B for Billionaires in America.

The short list, in no particular order includes:

Richard Branson
Ralph Lauren
Jenny Craig
Simon Cowell
Ted Turner
Steve Jobs
Rachel Ray
Barry Diller
Wayne Huizenga
Andrew Carnegie
Ingvar Kamprad (IKEA)
Debbi Fields
Coco Chanel
Mary Kay Ash (Mary Kay)
S. Daniel Abraham (Slim-Fast)
David Geffen
Dave Thomas
Giorgio Armani
Ty Warner (Beanie Babies and more)
Cornelius Vanderbilt
Larence J. Ellison
Michael Dell

Ray Kroc
Thomas Edison
Bill Gates
Paul Allen (Microsoft)
Frank Lloyd Wright
Milton Hershey
Asa Candler (Coca Cola)
Mark Zuckerberg
Howard Hughes
Walt Disney

And that's the short list, and remember B for Billionaire, not mortal millionaires.

There is an abundance of success and opportunity, just waiting for the taking. It's available to anyone who is hungry enough, determined enough, and courageous enough to reach out for it, and JUST GRAB IT!

You have to make it your burning desire to serve the betterment of mankind, to learn from everything, everyone, and every experience especially defeat, posses a willingness to burn all bridges of retreat, and not ever, ever stop trying, because defeat is not an option.

"A quitter never wins, and a winner never quits."

You will not always win, and defeat, or temporary failure is a prerequisite to success, but the ability to multiply your effort, your determination, your persistence, and continue to try, even when the world is mocking you, and in the face of defeat, is what makes all the difference.

Formal Education

Formal education can help you to get a job, and maybe even get your head high enough to peek out, above the heard, and see what is possible. But, the most important teacher, is life, and to be self educated in life's lessons.

There are many good professors but some are poisoning the minds of our youth, they are teaching business courses, without ever having spent a day running a business, meeting payroll, paying for an advertising campaign, making costly mistakes, or managing employees in the real world.

During my brief time as a Theater major, I read a book by David Mamet, writer of the hit movie Glengarry Glen Ross, among many others, and a Pulitzer Prize winner, he says:

"Most teachers, teach, because they can NOT do."

There are many wonderful teachers, that have done, and continue to do, but not all of them are wonderful, and some of them have only taught theory and metaphysical B.S. that doesn't last 15 minutes in the real world.

Listen, they are human beings, and must eat just like you and me. There is a professional athlete who speaks to grade schools, and tells kids not to listen to their teachers, especially when they say they can't do something.

Be selective with who you listen to, and what you listen to.

Gandhi, said to question everything including his own teachings. When you experience doubt, look within, search for the plain truth even if it reveals painful answers.

Examine the life of anyone who says you can't, what accomplishments have they made that qualifies them to say, you can't do it?

If you believe you can't do something, your almost always to be right!

Marconi, the italian inventor credited for the invention of the radio, was said to have been put in an insane asylum, when he first told his friends about radio (frequency) waves.

Did you know in a region of Columbia, there are doctors prescribing men to have intercourse with donkeys?

Newton discovered that white light was a result of all the colors of the rainbow, not by using a prism to look through, but by first poking his eye with a metal pole.

You don't have to know it all, and the funny thing about life is, the more you learn, the more you realize how little anyone knows about anything. When you accept this plain truth, you start to objectively see how even the smartest people, have said foolish things, through the course of history.

And your not likely to fare much better than, all of human existence, over all of recorded history. For, it wasn't that long ago, we thought the world was flat, and doctors sang of the health benefits of smoking tobacco, and claimed excessive masturbation caused you to go blind.

Chapter 4. Just Do It Now!

Let me give you the best piece of education, I would have liked earlier in my life, about waiting to learn, just finding a good teacher, or being shown how.

Go FIGURE IT OUT, and just do it ... right NOW!

This one skill is priceless.

The ability to go figure it out, and to have the willingness to be wrong, to be humiliated, and fail miserably. But you will try to do, and do it to the best of your current capabilities, is essential for achieving the good life.

Don't hold back or not give it your all, because it's your first time, or you haven't been shown how, and you didn't read the instruction manual. This book, and a few other good ones, are the closest thing you will ever get to an instruction manual in life.

This information should be required reading in all schools, along with how to effectively sell and market your products, small business, services. This is after all, how we all eat in a capitalist society, and it is the skill most equivalent to being able to hunt, in civilizations of the past.

The ability to go and get a job done, shows your a self starter, and good employers are aware that with every job, there are unexpected bumps on the road. In addition to many unplanned and expensive potholes on the road of even successful ventures.

Someone who is too fearful to get on the road, to make the best decision, or let alone any decision, once you have all the pertinent information, in the time you have, and be willing to be 100% wrong. Doesn't have a chance.

But, those folks who are decisive and want to try again when they do fail, because they're that much closer to figuring it out ... right now, this minute, today ... Instead, of merely thinking, dreaming, and wishing, it were easier!

These decisive individuals have cracked the code to success, even if they aren't conscious of using these tenets. For it's only a matter of time before the world makes way, and parts the seas, to deliver success to these driven folks.

Experience is the best teacher, and one sure fire path to figuring out the right way, is to first do it the wrong way! Brain Tracy said "Anything worth doing, is worth doing poorly at first, and often worth doing poorly, until you master it."

Learn Through Books

Books are some of the best sources of knowledge, as you've certainly already discovered reading this one. If you want something to judge someone by, do it by their library or lack of one.

People spend obscene amounts of money on gym memberships, vitamins, natural, and organic food for their body, but neglect to feed the most important part of the body, your mind!

For it is is equally valuable to feed your mind, new and exciting experiences, challenges, and learn new things. Along, with your body.

When you read, something unusual occurs, it can't fully be explained. It gives your brain away to rest, recoup, and break free from the bonds of everyday reality. It empowers your mind to soar and dream of the future, like it was designed to do.

A $100.00 investment in books has been infinitely more valuable to me in my career, than the $100,000.00, for my formal education.

"Good readers, are good leaders."

Learn From Other People

Learn, from other people. Learn from successful people, if there aren't any successful people in sight, you can still learn, just learn what not to do.

Jim Rohn says:

"It's too bad failures don't hold seminars, because they have a lot of valuable information to share. If you know someone who's failed in life, it may do some good to say hey John, can I spend the afternoon with you, your a good looking guy, every reason in the world to do well, how did you mess it all up!"

Jim Rohn, if your unfamiliar is one of the early mentors of Tony Robbins, and Jim, credits his philosophy in life, to having the opportunity to learn from Earl Shoaff, who said:

"If you wish to be successful, study success. If you wish to be happy, study happiness. If you want to make money, study the acquisition of wealth. Those who achieve these things don't do it by accident. It's a matter of studying first and practicing second."

I promise you, successful people will be willing to help you, once your truly committed and hungry to achieve. But, you sure can't wait for them to show you the first step, or maybe even the 30th step, but if you get started now, you will find an abundance of successful people willing to show you, and help you in your journey.

Remember, you must be willing to go the extra mile, and serve first. This means you must be willing to help someone else with what you know, without any expectation of receiving. Sharing our knowledge and our ability to fish, with a hungry fisherman, is living the good life.

It provides riches, often in material form, but also intangible riches. You will have a positive impact in the world, and these folks may go on to say you made all the difference in their life.

You'll know it was only showing them the path, they are responsible for taking it. Just as you and I are responsible for our success in life, wealth is attracted to responsibility.

If you haven't yet, make today, the day, you break free from the bonds of excuse making and start taking responsibility for your life, and current circumstances. Especially, if they aren't to your liking. For a plain truth is your the only one that can change these circumstances.

Often the first step is acknowledging your human and have flaws, because you see you can learn to do ANYTHING you really want to do, but you won't ever learn something you only wish to do.

Chapter 5. Be Like Mike

The major reason Michael Jordan will go down in history, as one of the greatest athlete's of all time and deservedly is because at the end of every season, he gathered up all the years of his basketball experience, and put them into getting better for the next season.

Michael worked, played, and exerted effort, everyday to get better including days to take physical rest, even after being titled scoring champion, MVP, and NBA champion.

For that is the only way, one could accomplish such an outstanding feat, as winning 6 NBA championships, and competing in professional baseball.

Listen, Michael experienced temporary setback, and failure. One thing the herd often graze by, is that the Chicago Bulls were defeated 3 years in row, in the playoffs, by the Detroit Pistons.

And Michael, had to first invest time getting better himself, and at using the strengths of his teammates, before the team stood victoriously, trophy in hand, and chests filled with pride. Very similar to Lebron James of today.

Live your life, the same way Michael, and Lebron play basketball. Get better every single day, and get better at recognizing, praising, and sharing your love and laughter with others, especially your family!

Be fascinated with life, and determined that you will make your square block in life, fit through the round hole of success. Carry the same determination toddlers have, as you make yourself attractive to success and wealth.

Mistakes

Doing something wrong, is one of the best opportunities to learn. There is no substitute for the experience of costly mistakes. I've learned making costly mistakes is the quickest way for me to learn ANYTHING.

Make sure you learn the lesson, or else you'll be liable to make the the same mistakes, over and over again.

A common mistake among the herd, is to simply go through life and carry the belief that their employment is like fine red wine, and with age it becomes more valuable. These folks will often run off to their employer, and demand more money, for simply working and repeating another year.

You can only be fine red wine, if you learn something new in that year, and can bring more skills and value, today. The skills, and the attitude in which you perform your duties, is essential to any promotion, and increase in earnings in a job, and for any business.

The idea that just because you are willing to repeat the same functions, for another year, doesn't in and of itself make you any more valuable. You have to make yourself irreplaceable to an employer and customers.

"You must learn more, in order to earn more!"

Your attitude is big here. Just think for a moment, I'm sure your not interested in spending your money at an unappreciative business. This is true with people too, no one wants to be helped by a nasty salesman, who is a victim of existing, and carries an infectious negative personality.

We all however, do want someone who will go the extra mile to help us and is smiling and without complaining, even if they have to figure out how to do it. And employers love finding a superstar, who will take the initiative to do a job, without needing to be told, and do a good job.

Repetition

The more you do anything the better you get. If you want to be successful, take actions measure your progress, make course corrections, and take more actions!

Continuously, repeat, and reexamine your goals, the progress your making, and read the good books, over and over again!

Learning is just like personal development, it is a lifelong process, that should never end! This is the path to growth, and not simply repeating one year over, and over, and over again.

Chapter 6. The X Factor

Look, other people give life richness, value, and purpose, but isn't it interesting that other people are at the same time one of the greatest sources of criticism, hypocrisy, and negativity.

One of the great discoveries in life is the yin and yang and the universal balance. Law enforcement agencies must have criminals to chase, teachers must have students, leaders must have followers.

It is one of the great mysteries in life but the herd, distract themselves into living in a delusional nice world filled with leprechauns riding unicorns along rainbows.

Certainly, you have a friend that sounds like a broken record always saying they need to do blank, have to stop doing something, and just spin their wheels never actually doing anything!

Or worse, they are overflowing with hypocrisy. It took me a long time to learn this, but the people that scream the loudest, are the first you should ignore.

In addition, to the fact the guy clamoring about being honest is who you should really watch out for!

Do you recall a few years back a TV evangelist banging his drum about how homosexuality is a sin, but behind closed doors he was found to being using meth in the company of male escorts.

How about the politician in Washington who was arrested for cocaine? You must have heard about the mayor of Toronto?

One big kicker about this so called war on drugs, is one the most drug infested neighborhoods in America is located in Washington D.C. within a stone's throw of the capital building, Hanover Place, and drug kingpin Cornell Jones.

The funniest of all, Kim Jong II the great leader of North Korea, was a fan of Michael Jordan and the Chicago Bulls. Madeline Albright, even delivered him an autographed Basketball.

You've heard that saying about throwing bricks when you live in a glass house?

Yet, it happens all the time! The recent AA member is the first person screaming about his friend Jack's drinking problem. This unfortunately is a plain truth of life.

It's good to look at what people do, and have done, and not just what they say. Don't forget appearances are often deceptive. Just as Dr. Phil says one of the greatest indicators and predictors of what someone will do in the future, is what they did yesterday.

It's true, people can change, but rarely are they really willing to actually do what it takes to change. At the same time every day, and every moment, we are always changing.

You're either taking steps to building success and the good life, or continuing to stumble down the traveled road of dilution, strengthening the bonds and habits of frustration, failure, and poverty.

The small minority of folks who do rise above the herd, are continuously on the watch to change, and grow in this journey, we call life. They think big picture especially when it comes to wealth, instead of chasing the latest fads, do-hickeys, and getting the newest model of the iPhone.

You see, the herd seems to relish in chasing silver bullets and choosing to live in a groundhog day existence. The popular book The Millionaire Next Door, does a splendid job showing how 20 years ago in the herd, the adult child is often chasing the latest SUV, counting and spending his inheritance before receiving it, and living a life of silver bullet quick fixes.

Look, success is not an easy path, a glamorous path, or what the media are interested in portraying. It is however, the path to being genuinely happy, successful, and enjoying your life, instead of investing your happiness in the latest celebrity sex scandal, who wins the Super Bowl, and the top 10 SportsCenter plays.

Come ON MAN!

The Critics

Have you ever felt like the world, was just waiting for you to mess up?

The plain truth, is it's true. Go to a college basketball game, there are 20,000 people eagerly sitting on their hands, just waiting for a player to shoot an air ball, just like a great big bulldog drooling, and waiting to sink his teeth, into a fluffily, soft bunny rabbit, and tear it to shreds.

The dog won't stop or come up for a breath, and people are exactly the same, for those courageous soul's who rise to the challenge and dare to peek out, above the herd.

Look at all the Monday morning quarterbacks, who criticize teams, even when they win!

Listen, the people that criticize, are the spectators in life. Their waiting for the stars to align and are busy investing in this weeks lottery tickets, to do anything productive for their life.

When you get criticism from the herd, remember, your playing in the game and they're merely spectating. For they ought to be careful, I hear too much time sitting on the pine, can result in a splinter, in your butt!

The plain truth is your going to mess up, you will stumble, you will have egg on your face, and for the super achiever it will happen over and over and over again.

A secret to success is it takes this willingness, just to play in the game. The herd may criticize you, judge you, and condemn you, but behind your back they will sing your name in praise, and look enviously upon your success.

Listen, the people who matter don't mind what you do, so long as your not violating the rights of man, and the people who mind really don't matter!

Think back to the weakest, winiest, crybaby kid you knew growing up, for me it was a friend we will call Peter. You see Peter was a big wussy. He would run home to his Mom and his

Mom would go out and fight all of Peter's battles.

Decades later and Peter, still lives with his Mommy, but now he uses hard drugs, has a drinking problem, and is the one who just left some atrociously nasty comment about your product, or service, because his Mommy said she wasn't going to continue to finance his nudie magazine day.

Sure, Peter!

You see, successful people aren't going to waste their time, criticizing you, or anyone for that matter, sharing criticism serve's nobody any good. Those that do criticize are those folks with abundant time, talking of fairness, worrying about aliens attacking, and not missing Gerry Springala's talk show this afternoon.

Teddy Roosevelt's sister, Auntie Bye, once told Eleanor:

"Never be bothered by what people say, as long as you know in your heart, you are right."

Listen, the critical Peter's in the world, are everywhere. They are at your job, in your families, among your friends.

It is imperative that you eliminate these people from your life, and if that's not possible, minimize their influence. These are the kids that were bullies in grade school, because their Mommy didn't love them enough.

The only thing that changed is they grew up, and now have the vocabulary of a slightly advanced chimpanzee, with the profanity of a sailor.

They regularly engage in the sin of envy and lash out at you, because of the circumstances in their life, their insecurities, their shortcomings. Don't be a fool and let Peter, stop you from playing in the game of life!

Do you hear that ringing? For it sounds to me, that the southern baptist church bells are ringing with the gospel on this plain truth.

Chapter 7. Gene Autry Country Music Star

Take a lesson from Gene Autry, and the great military leaders of the past, and keep your lines of supply open.

The country music star, Gene Autry, tells the story of working for Frisco Railways, in small town, Chelsea, Oklahoma.

When one night he was playing and singing cowboy songs, and Gene was told by a traveler that he was good, and ought to pursue a career with it.

This traveler said he should go out to New York City and pursue this path, only later did

Gene discover this traveler was none other than Will Rogers.

Here's the kicker, Gene Autry didn't go at once, he didn't quit his job, and run to New York City.

Gene kept open his supply lines.

He first, spent 9 months just thinking about it, then decided to go for it. But, Gene didn't walk into a recording studio, and lay down a platinum record, or star in a Blockbuster movie.

On his first trip to New York City, he couldn't even find a job but, because he kept open his supply lines, he returned to his job with the Railway, saved some money, and then went out to New York City, to try again.

Only through a series of what the herd call "lucky breaks" and "being in the right place at the right time" over the course of a few years, did Gene eventually find himself starring in Hollywood pictures and being one of the biggest stars in country music and film.

You can see how Gene Autry, wasn't chasing some pie in the sky dreams, with a bunch of impulsive, hair brained plans, that were about as serious as most folks New Years Resolutions.

Instead, he was smart, made calculated decisions, and continued to work for what he wanted, by putting himself in a position for good things to happen, along with keeping open his lines of supply, and consequently food in his stomach.

However, while this is the smart path, it is certainly not the only path. Sylvester Stalone spent time sleeping in New York City bus stations, before getting his big break, which coincidentally was a role in an adult film. There's a dose of fairness for you.

Here are just a few other celebrities that were at one point without a home, food, and those basic necessities, that we take for granted, almost everyday of our life.

Jim Carrey, William Shatner, Halle Berry, David Letterman, Dr. Phil, Tyler Perry, Hilary Swank, Drew Carrey, and a whole laundry list of more folks.

And these are just a few of the famous, celebrities, we're not even looking at the "real world people" and the folks that fought through failure, setback, and defeat, over and over and over again!

Did you know Walt Disney, P.T. Barnum, David Buick, James Folger, Henry Ford, Conrad Hilton, J.C. Penney, Sam Walton, H.J. Heinz, William Fox, Milton Hershey, Larry King, Dave Ramsey, Stan Lee, and even George Foreman all experienced bankruptcy before they achieved their significant fortunes, and success.

Earl Nightingale talks of taking his son out to see a coral reef, on a vacation in the Caribbean islands. The coral on the ocean side of the reef was vibrant, full of energy, and life-like, were as the coral on the protected side of the reef, looked dead and lifeless.

When they asked the tour guide why this was, he told them, the reef on the ocean side, were constantly challenged, battling the ocean waves, and were thus most alive! The coral needed to overcome. And we human beings aren't much different!

Michael Jordan, said he needed the doubters, the criticism, and people saying he couldn't do it! It feels good to prove someone wrong, and you know that saying about success being the sweetest revenge, it's true!

When the last grain of sand drains from your hourglass in life, do you want to look back and see a life full of worry, regret, and wish you had just gotten started, or taken the first step and tried to figure it out?

Or do you want to look back and see a rich life, that was truly lived, overflowing with incredible experiences, sharing time with loved ones, expressing thankfulness for all the moments you've be given, and seeing how you were making all the little right choices over the course of your life to bring you to today, instead of the little momentary poor decisions that build a life full of regret.

The Right Time

Look, the herd go through life waiting for the right time to act, waiting for the perfect alignment of the stars, but on the rare instance, the stars do line up, and the circumstances are right, they're too busy, watching Dr. Phil's talk show, and Tyler Perry's latest movie!

This is because action is uncomfortable. It requires you to grow, learn, and use effort. This is what the herd calls "hard work." This is the labor and it creates new life, as Jim Rohn says, and I assure you it is true!

This is my 7th book, the first 6 continue to create an abundance of new life, new customers, new website visitors, heck, even fan mail. Not to mention helping many other hungry fisherman learn how to fish, and at the same time helping myself.

Chapter 8. The Midas Touch

Look, the herd may call it good genes, disposition, charisma, confidence, or even god given talent to be an outgoing, social magnet, and naturally command the attention, and admiration of the other members in our herd.

The plain truth is this skill, is just like everything else, and 90% of it is learned through practice, repetition, and experimentation. One required ingredient includes a genuine desire to help and serve other people.

It is truly worth investing even a minimal amount of time, studying primate behavior. I've found it to be very helpful applying it to human behavior and it makes finding an explanation for the other monkeys behavior, much easier to find.

A dirty little secret, of the herd, is Homer and everyone human being is a giant ball of insecurities. On a typical day Homer is worrying about being replaced at work by a machine or a monkey living in a 3rd world country, who Homer claims doesn't even speak American.

His most pressing concern, is if Marge bought his lottery tickets, and if he'll get stuck in "Happy Hour" traffic at the bar, or make it home in time to catch Gerry Springala, and the mega million dollar sweepstakes drawing.

It is imperative that you create a positive impression when you cross paths with Homer and even Michael Scott and Dwight Schrute of the The Office. It's key to be overflowing with kindness, compassion, friendliness, understanding, and actually listen to them, if even for a moment. It is a source of knowledge and someone you can learn from.

It was once said by a very wealthy man:

"The herd goes through life, frantically searching with their umbilical cord in hand hoping to find someone to hook it up to, and it often pays handsomely, to put yourself in a position, to be this person."

I'm not going to dig into this statement to much, but certainly you can see the application in many facets of life. It's a good premise to follow, to help you create that winning charisma with your professional and personal life.

Growing up, I attended five different high schools and I assure you this midas touch with other people is something that can be learned, even if it is learned only from necessity.

It's a skill I continue to work on, and polish decades later. Please, don't be that fool, who says I've already read Dale Carnegie's How To Win Friends and Influence People, that should be a regular read for everyone.

The Golden Rule

Yes, please practice the golden rule, and really listen, to other people. This is one of the most effective ways of learning from others, and take the lessons you can from what they do right and wrong, along with asking them questions about their journey in life.

The action of getting excited about someone else's accomplishments, paying them a genuine compliment, and encouragement, is the food and energy we get from other people. We human beings feed off one another, both the good and bad. This is why negativity, misery, and fear are so contagious, and deadly to your well being.

The people, you spend time with, influence you tremendously. Choose carefully who you associate with and who you spend your time around.

Don't misplace your values or confidences, and remember, Homer is the same ape, who was just stomping around frustrated because he just discovered that life isn't fair.

It's a good habit when you see Homer, look for his best quality and praise it, you will be planting the seeds for him to grow.

Keep quiet about any of his short comings. I assure you, he is his own worst critic, and may need to substitute living in a delusional world if only to continue his existence on earth.

Accept him as he is, just as if you were buying a used car, faults and all. Only though the journey of life, does your body collect dings, scratches, and scrapes.

It's only natural for Homer to look at your beautifully maintained, automobile through life, and be envious, and look back with regret for not having taken better care of his own. This is the well traveled road in life.

Chapter 9. No Excuses

There is no excuse for not doing well in our brave new world, despite what the politicians and talking heads on TV claim, and may even believe.

You see, there is an endless array of opportunities and technologies, that provide you and I, the ability to create and build recurring passive income streams, even on a part-time basis, and from home.

Look, no longer do you need to take a sabbatical or quit your job, like Martha Stewart did, to launch your career. Instead, you can follow John Grisham's path and write your first book part-time, while you continue to work a full-time job and continue earning money so you can eat.

The truth with excuses, is they are reasons why you aren't willing to do what it takes to be successful. These excuses are justifications, for not doing more.

If you can honestly look yourself in the mirror and say that it's Mr. Burns fault, today, and be OK with saying that to yourself toward the end of your life, then by all means feel free.

I would suggest you try thinking of any one of the many reasons, why you can and will succeed. When I look at the excuses I used in the past ranging from the credit crisis, the government, taxes, Joe, and because it's Monday. None of these stand up against the test of time! They are all weak excuses for me not doing what it takes before!

Excuse making is a habit, and one that you must overcome to achieve success.

Time with Little Things

Please, don't waste your time with the little things! Your energy is so much more valuable. People are people, we get ourselves so worked up when strangers cut us off on the freeway, people are rude, and our friends or family members, wrong us.

Unfortunately, other people make mistakes, just like you and I have, and will continue to. We're human.

Judas betrayed Jesus, in the worst way, why should you and I expect better results in our life.

You only have three choices, you can end your friendship or relationship, you can say something about it if their is the possibility of desirable results, or let it go.

But, sitting around and talking about how you can't believe Becky said your butt looks big, and holding a grudge is a big, giant, stinking pile of wasted energy.

Our brain uses about 25% of our daily energy, that's a lot! Make sure, that energy is invested in constructive use, and not complaining about something that can't be changed.

The milk is spilled, let's go ahead and clean it up.

You will encounter many unreasonable, unfair, and non ideal people, and situations in your journey through life.

But, you only harm yourself, and further their agenda, when you hold a grudge, or spend your time thinking or talking about how they wronged you.

Make sure, you don't let these potholes in life, get you off track. Stay focused, do what you can, learn what you can, and forget it!

Did you know Earl Nightingale was only 1 of 15 marines, that survived the bombing of Pearl Harbor?

Earl didn't spend the rest of his life, escaping with drugs and alcohol, bemoaning his emotional turmoil, hating those individuals that killed his comrades, or allow this catastrophic event to prevent him from living the good life, a life filled with value, satisfaction, happiness, and service to others.

He got on with it, and let it go. He is a shining example of the good life, and why treating every human being as a brother, sister, mother, daughter, and member of the human family, regardless of race, gender, nationality, religion, and creed is so important to helping ourself. We all must live in this world together.

If your unfamiliar, Earl grew up in severe poverty during the depression. When his Dad abandoned the family, they moved into a tent! Earl went on to greatness, amassing a vast fortune, and creating a brand new industry, you may recognize him from such programs as "The Strangest Secret" and "Lead The Field."

Live In The Truth

You have to be able, willing, and choose to look at the world and search for the plain truths in life.

There have been, and always will be an endless number of people in the world, promising easy answers, and giving you someone to blame. This is nothing more than delusion!

Don't allow yourself to be diluted into believing these claims! Like it or not, you are where you are today, as a result of your choices.

It's better to be able to see reality, and be willing to recognize your faults, weaknesses, and shortcomings, so you can get busy changing and improving yourself immediately.

Beware the religious fanatics, politicians, and anyone that tears something down without first building an alternative. It's good to keep a healthy dose of skepticism, but don't be too cynical of everything and everyone, or else you may miss out on some amazing experiences.

Truths With Work

Listen, no job is perfect especially if your working for yourself. The path of entrepreneurship, requires you to do every job, and be willing to do any job at any time, under any circumstances.

The things your weak at and don't require your attention, can and should be delegated, but you still must manage, even if a few layers removed. Every task you delegate must be managed.

Selling should never be delegated exclusively, or else you may not continue to stay in business or have sales.

The point here is, simply there are parts of every job that are not ideal. The idea of doing only what one is passionate about is sheer foolishness.

The plain truth is the only people I've meet that can't get passionate about earning money, are those that have yet to be hungry and broke!

Most often those claiming they don't feel passionate for a job, are looking for easy answers to complex questions. In other words, they may talk about how badly they want success, but they aren't willing to do much more than talk about it.

This is also a friendly reminder, to always be courteous and give everyone dignity, you may be doing their job tomorrow if you weren't yesterday.

We aren't necessarily better than others because the gospel of success show us, if not for the grace of god there could be you and I holding a sign that reads will work for food.

Be courteous, give dignity, compassion, and understanding to everyone, regardless of where they are, or what job they are performing, be reasonable!

Chapter 10. Your Influence

One of the plain truths in life is you will influence people, especially those that are closest to you. We all have the most impact and influence with our family members and everyone with whom we cross paths.

It is up to you if you want your influence to be positive or negative. You may be surprised to hear, this influence is how other people will remember you.

Do you really want to be someone that is looking for all the faults, shortcomings, and fatal flaws in other people and in your life?

I guarantee if you are, life will not disappoint! You do however have a choice.

You see, there are some people who love life, they are eager to jump out of bed ready to face the day's challenges. And the big difference between this zest for living and dreading another Monday, is what you invest your time thinking about and programming into your subconscious.

The bottom line is, at any given time, in every human beings life, about 80% of circumstances are majestic, and about 20% of things could be better. You can choose which aspect you want to focus your time and energy on. I would encourage you to choose all the stuff going right!

Life has a way of delivering to us exactly what it is we expect of and from it.

Michael Jordan says one of the most important things he wants to pass along to his kids is to always expect the best! Expect the best for yourself and be smart enough to know that you're going to have to learn through life.

You will have to put in effort and time, this is what most people call hard work, but I don't see my work as being hard. It does require effort but it is fun, enjoyable, and very rewarding!

Be a Winner

Dr. Maxwell Maltz, author of the book Psycho-Cybernetics and one of the first plastic surgeons in our country, discovered that people must feel good on the inside, in order to ever feel as though they look good on the outside.

It is of the utmost importance that you continuously work on building your self-confidence, through life.

You can make magic happen, just like Walt Disney did, after he went bankrupt. You see whatever your burning desire is in life, you can achieve it! Someone else has probably already done it, and if not someone will do it.

We know Buzz Aldrin and Neil Armstrong because they were the first men to walk on the moon, but they haven't been the only men, and there were a number of other men that had they beaten them there, we would know their name instead.

Remember, success is not the easy path, which is one BIG reason why everyone else isn't taking this path.

Don't neglect to laugh and smile your way though life, and live only for today. Plan for tomorrow, share yesterday, but live today. Every 24 hour day is the Super Bowl in our game of life.

Invest some time playing with kids, they are the best. Try to see yourself the way kids see you! My splendid little nephew sees his Uncle Dan as pretty darn awesome, and super fun!

Please, do take time to listen to kids. Kids are some of the best sources of knowledge. They don't have any filters and are much less influence from the herd and society as a whole. Furthermore, kids will often only speak the plain truth!

Chapter 11. Be Kind Rewind

The most important aspect here is not only to be kind to other people, but also be kindest to yourself. Many folks go through life creating and trying to live by unreasonable standards.

You have to love yourself more than a parent loves their child. You have to give yourself all the love, support, nourishment, and give that out to the rest of the world, because most folks need some. Everybody is a member of the human family and someone's brother, mother, sister, cousin, aunt, and friend.

Why some people choose to do bad things is one of the great mysteries of life. I'm confident that it is a result of not receiving enough kindness during their life, and being unable to give this precious gift to themselves.

Not sure, how else folks can choose to throw their life away with destructive habits.

Enthusiasm

Enthusiasm is a required ingredient to sell anything. And remember all through life, even if you're not selling products or services, you're still selling your ideas to your friends and family members.

When you act enthusiastic with high energy and with a genuine desire to help other people, you become magnetic to other people, magnetic to success, opportunity, and wealth.

Understanding

Frequently, people go through life judging everything and everyone. But judging other people is easy to do. It is much more difficult to try and understand other people, even criminals, and what type of a life went into making the poor decisions that have created their results.

Reasonableness

Be reasonable with the world. Don't be a victim. Everyone has hardships, and difficult times in life, you can either learn, grow, and change yourself or waste your life waiting for the world to change.

Being a victim of circumstances and trying to change the world is futile. The plain truth is you don't have to change the world, but it is a good practice to take action to change yourself in order to achieve the life you really want.

Nature is unforgiving, it doesn't matter if you do or don't change because either way life will continue to move forward. Nature doesn't wait for anything or anyone!

Make a stand, draw a line in the sand, and do whatever it takes to succeed and create the reality you really want in your life. One of the secrets keys to life, is to stay grounded and focused as you go through the peeks and valleys in the roller-coaster of life.

Balance

There is a delicate balance that must be found, in order to live a truly rich life. This is the balance between work and play, pain and pleasure, love and hate, sweet-and-sour. You must have both and often times experience with both, in order to enjoy and appreciate the good.

Urgency

You must have some urgency to make your life happen right now. Chances are it'll take some time, especially if your just getting started. Chances are you'll do a few things right and a few things wrong.

But, if you don't get started and get busy right now and instead wait until tomorrow, it will only be more difficult to begin and to follow through to achievement.

Chapter 12. The Stone Tablet

Look, hands down the most valuable plain truth in life, and what your future holds, lies written on your stone tablet.

You see, we humans are all governed by our tablet, this tablet is sometimes called your ego, self esteem, confidence, automatic success mechanism, and a host of other synonyms. It is how you see yourself!

What can you see yourself doing?

Do you see your life filled with abundance, happiness, wealth, harmony, love ... do you see yourself as a one of a kind masterpiece, with immense value to share and help other people with?

The low achievers in life, those that supposedly have potential to do something, but never actualize on any of their capabilities. These folks are the masses, the herd, the majority of humans. It's not that they don't want to achieve, or be successful. In fact they are the most desperate for these things!

It's a revelation of success, the potential winners but actual losers in life, the low achievers, high complainers, criticizers, whiners, cry babies, and finger pointers, don't achieve because of their tablet. Some nasty caregiver, sibling, friend, associate at some point in their life wrote in big capital letters that this person wasn't deserving, couldn't achieve, and instead they were destined to remain a loser!

It's most unfortunate, for you see, every adult was once a magnificent child, with the whole world, and his entire future in front of him!

His future can be as big and as bright as he can dream! It is ONLY because these dark influences of other people, and the daggers of criticism came down upon this child and eventually when you tell someone something long enough, it is possible for them to accept this false belief.

This is what criticism does to the herd! Most people are so wounded and understandably so, by what their supposed loved ones said, they never even reach for their dreams!

How else can you explain why people stay in physically or emotionally abusive relationships? It's hard to do good things, when you don't feel you deserve good things in your life!

For you see, every generation must have a class of success, there must be the someone that is the next president of our country, the next Lebron James, the next Earl Nightingale, the next Michael Phelps, the next Justin Timberlake, the next Mark Cuban, and the next Warren Buffett.

The ONLY question is if that will be you? And if not you, then who? For someone must be in these positions, it's just a matter of who will it be?

Go now and grab a copy your free bonus gift of the 12 week success course at DanMoskelUniversity.com

Other Books by Dan Moskel

- *Entrepreneur Bible To Riches: The Gospel of Wealth Attraction*

- *Video Marketing for Entrepreneurs*

- *Email Marketing That Works ... So You Don't Have To*

- *How To Create a Website Easy Button: Earn Money Online with Google AdSense, Amazon, Your Business, and More*

- *SEO Training Manual - The 10 Golden Steps To Shower In Search Engine Traffic*

- *The Blueprint To Affiliate Marketing: Revealed My Exact Million Dollar Earning Strategies Tips and Tricks*

www.ingramcontent.com/pod-product-compliance
Lightning Source LLC
Chambersburg PA
CBHW051817170526
45167CB00005B/2051